The
PASSIONATE
Life

A COMMON MAN'S GUIDE
To Getting Everything You Want
Out of Anything You Do

Mitche Graf

Mitche Graf

The Passionate Life
Copyright © 2009 by Mitche Graf

For wholesale orders or corporate gift purchases please visit www.thepassionatelifebook.com

Cover Photo: Mark Huender
Cover Design: Susan Cegerra
Back Cover Photo: Craig Kienast
Editor: Alan M. Perlman, Ph.D.
Assistant Editor: Robyn Wright

Publisher: GrafCorp International
888.544.4149

ISBN #978-0-615-27553-6

Dedication

This book is dedicated to my father, George Alan Graf, who taught me to love the outdoors and to appreciate Mother Nature and all she has to offer. Most of my *"bright ideas"* and writings have taken place in outdoor settings, and it's because of his encouragement and support that this has been possible.

So to my Dad, I say *THANK YOU*, and *I LOVE YOU!*

Table of Contents

About the Author...vi

1. The Birth of Passion 1

2. Finding *Your* Passion... 5

3. What Keeps Us From Being Passionate? 19

4. What I Offer You—the Passionate Life............................ 31

5. Passion as the Fuel for Our Journey 41

6. Busy-Ness and Focus, Sharpening the Axe 49

7. Taking Responsibility... 61

8. The Importance of Humor: Lighten Up! 73

9. Goals and the Power of the Dream 83

10. What You Make of It 89

11. Taking Action 99

12. Traits of the Ultra-Passionate 107

13. Mitche's 5-Step Program 117

14. Summing It Up 129

About the Author

Internationally renowned speaker and author Mitche Graf has been passionately involved in the field of sales and marketing for over twenty-five years and has ventured into many exciting businesses along the way. From selling used bicycle parts out of the garage in the seventh grade to running four companies today, he has prided himself on knowing how to maximize each and every business he has been involved with.

In the past, he has owned and operated several different businesses in a variety of industries including a cribbage board company, several manufacturing companies, a limousine business, a restaurant, a portable hot tub rental business, a drive-through espresso business, as well as consulting companies in several industries. He has learned that the basic principles of business are the same regardless of whether you are selling meat, corn, or bricks... *YOU MUST LOVE WHAT YOU DO!*

Through his successes and failures, Mitche has continued to make bold attempts to redefine the limits of his abilities, and a majority of his lessons have been learned from the School of Hard Knocks.

He firmly believes that life is meant to be lived …. not endured, and we each have the ability to make a difference in the world. He loves his family, loves his friends … and the rest just falls into place!

He is passionate about the outdoors … and about laughing, playing guitar, reading, listening to great music, cooking and eating, drinking good wine, taking time off, and most importantly spending time with his family.

Mitche lives in a small town in Oregon with his wife Tami and their two small children, Jaycee and Colton, as well as his blind black lab Manna, a mutt named Mooka, and several hundred guppies. Mitche spends much of his time looking for ways to work smarter and not harder, so he can spend more time doing the things in life that are most important to him.

CHAPTER 1

The Birth of Passion

Passion: *A powerful emotion, a strong desire, boundless enthusiasm, an abandoned display of excitement.*

I believe life takes on all sorts of different meanings when you begin to tap into having a vision, or a dream, or a purpose. Let me tell you how I know this.

I can remember the day my daughter Jaycee was born back in 2005 almost as if it were yesterday. The moment I held her for the very first time and looked into her deep blue eyes, I instantly knew my life would never be the same.

All of a sudden, every ounce of my soul became transformed into much more than a husband, or a friend, or a co-worker, or a brother, or a son. I became a Daddy!

The Passionate Life

In the blink of an eye, everything that was once important in my life became secondary to taking care of this little human being that was totally dependent on me for everything. My sense of purpose became laser sharp.

I had waited 43 years to get married for the first time, and another two years to have my first child, so I had become pretty set in my ways, or as my wife tells me, "stubborn" in my ways. Then, when my son Colton came along two years later, it happened to me all over again!

The best part about little children is that they don't care how much money you make, or how expensive your car is, or who you know, or where you go on vacation, or how good of a golfer you are. All they care about is being loved and spending time with you.

Since then, I have worked diligently to reinvent and re-prioritize the way my life is put together.

- ❖ I want to work less so I can spend more time with my kids.
- ❖ I want to work smarter so I can spend more time with my kids.
- ❖ I want to find ways to become more efficient with my time so I can spend more time with my kids.
- ❖ I want to reinvent the way I do business so I can spend more time with my kids.
- ❖ I want to work less, and play more!

I have always approached my life head on with a full head of steam and at times was like a bull in a china shop! But one thing I can say about my philosophy is that you only live this life once, and you had better make it count!

The zest and zeal for living that I have always possessed in my guts have been there for as long as I can remember, but nothing compares to that feeling of complete joy you get when your child is born. I still have a long list of passions in my life, but my kids take the cake!

And now, I'm more determined than ever to live life like I mean it!

CHAPTER 2

Finding *Your* Passion

Can you tell me what the following numbers are?

- ❖ 1825-1877
- ❖ 1776-1851
- ❖ 1962- 2003

They are life spans. There's a born-on date and a dead-on date. We have very little control over either one of those, but what we do have control over is what we do with the time in between. It's called the "dash"—that little thing in between. It's everything that happens from the second you are born to the moment you die. It's your ENTIRE LIFE! The question that I would like you to marinate in your mind while you are reading this book is How are you spending your dash?

The "dash" is all you have to leave behind when you are done with your time on earth. Are you making a difference in the lives of the people who mean the most to you? Are you leaving behind a legacy of kindness and goodness? Do you wish you had more control over your life than you do today? Then this book was written for you!

When you are done reading this book, I want you to have a new set of eyes for what your true purpose in life is and to gain a renewed perspective on what's really important.

Loving the GAP

Another way of describing the "in-between" segment of your life is the "gap." Here's where you are, and there's where you want to be, and then there's the "gap." We need to learn to LOVE the gap, because that's where most of our life is lived—in a state of change. "Gap thinking" will help you understand the importance of your "dash."

What drives you to get out of bed every morning? Is it the drive to be a good parent, a dependable worker, a great friend, a caring and compassionate human being? We all want to be better Dads, Moms, friends, and workers. Yet success, or perhaps I should say happiness, eludes most people in this world. They're mired in jobs they hate, loveless marriages, and other quagmires. We all need something to strive for, to work towards, and dream about.

What's your reason for getting out of bed every day? If you can't come up with a better reason than "I have to," then I hope you'll take a good, hard look at your life.

Understanding Who You Are

Having an intimate understanding of what makes you tick is not only important to any type of business you may be involved with, but it is also vital to your life! To know your strengths, your weaknesses, and what challenges and excites you, you need to be in touch with all of these things to be the best you can be. In other words, you must make sure your creative juices are constantly being swished around inside your soul so you know what you want out of your life.

Let's compare your creative juices to a car with a full tank of gas. At the beginning of a trip you feel pretty good, driving down the road looking at all the sights, excited and enthused about your journey and not too concerned with what lies ahead.

As the miles go by, the needle starts to drop and you start thinking about filling up, but the next gas station isn't for another 100 miles! So . . . you continue driving. If you don't get gas soon, you will end up stranded on the side of the road! Now, would you let your gas tank get so low you run the risk of running it dry in the middle of nowhere? So why would you allow your brain to run for long periods of time without adding fuel to its tank?

The fuel for your brain must come in the form of your creative juices and mental energy! Nobody else has the desire to make you succeed as much as you.

I have some friends that walked away from a very lucrative business after twenty-five years in the same industry because they were burned out by doing the same things over and over, dealing with the same people, selling the same products, doing the same job every day, day after day. They were making a great living, had lots of toys and seemed to have a good time with their business. I was talking with them one day, and they informed me that they had lost the fun many years before and had simply been going through the motions for quite some time.

For all of their adult lives, they had only known one job, so getting situated in a new field didn't come easy. After about a year, they both grew anxious and began to realize how much they actually missed their old gig! They quit their jobs and went back into business.

But before they did, they had plenty of opportunity to research new and different ways of just about everything relating to the running of their business. This actually began to become quite enjoyable for them, and before long, they had developed a head of steam that has allowed them to totally and completely reinvent the way their business operates.

What a joy it has been to watch their new business grow from the bottom up all over again and to see them discover new and exciting ways of conducting their business. It's almost like they are going into business for the very first time . . . and it's because they allowed themselves the creative freedom to brainstorm for a breakthrough. In doing so, they found their passion.

Is this something that sounds intriguing to you? Do you have the desire to reinvent your life and re-energize your creative juices? Brainstorming, by yourself or with others, can give you the opportunity!

By brainstorming and jotting down ideas, thoughts, and feelings, you begin to know yourself better, and you can go back over your life and look at how you've grown. You can recapture experiences that shaped you into the person you are today. I'll talk more about this later.

This is an important process. There is an innate desire deep inside each of us to reach for goals that seem unreachable. I'm talking about those hopes and dreams we all have. Some are lying just below the surface, but some have been so deeply buried for so long that it will take time to dig them out. It's our nature to have something to move toward all the time.

If someone asked us, we would readily acknowledge we want life to be exciting, but some of us have gotten too comfortable and content sitting on our respective couches of life. We need a challenge, but only a few of us ever dare to follow our hearts.

The Passionate Life

Identifying Your Motives: What Really Drives You?

It's sad to say that most people never slow down long enough to ask themselves why they are doing what they are doing. What are your motives? Maybe it's the hope of a promotion at work, or the encouragement we get from a spouse or close friend, or for the safety and nurturing of our children.

Real love is a big motivator for me. I'm not talking about the kind of love you have for a double cheeseburger with fries, or having affection for your favorite team, or a good book at night. I'm talking about pure, unadulterated love that can only come from a pure heart. If you are a parent, you know exactly what I mean. The kind of love that would drive you to do anything, and I mean anything, to make sure your children are safe, protected, and well taken care of.

My grandparents were married for over fifty years before my grandmother recently passed away, but every time I saw them together, they would be holding hands as if it were the first time. It made my heart melt every time I saw them.

Another motivator is success. If you are an entrepreneur, the drive to succeed is a strong motivator. You have an idea or a dream, and through hard work and determination, that dream slowly begins to take on a life of its own. We work day in and day out to build something that not only will create an income but will provide needed goods and services to the world, provide jobs for local people, and give us a feeling of accomplishment.

Taking an idea and breathing life into its belly, then watching that idea become something that you and the world can be proud of gives you an incredible feeling. Anyone who owns a business undoubtedly has a list of personal motivators.

The Passionate Life

Motivation: What Really Drives Our Action?

I waited until I was in my forties before getting married for the first time and having kids. The very instant my kids were born, my motivations instantly changed. All of a sudden, my entire existence was wrapped around thoughts of being a good dad, a good husband and provider, being the best person I could be for my children. In many respects, I grew up as soon as I saw their precious faces. My motivators changed, and so did my attitude towards what I was doing with my life.

Some people are motivated by doing good things for others, like volunteering at the local homeless shelter or helping out at the annual Elks Christmas Basket fundraiser. Some people are fulfilled simply by bringing a smile to someone's face.

Some people are motivated by all sorts of negative factors such as revenge, bitterness, jealousy, insecurity, or fear.

These motivators, whether positive or negative, are the very fuel for our car. They're the force that drives us every day, and it's important for us to have a handle on what makes us tick. Sit down and list some of the motivators you have for doing what you do. We all have a list, as if there's an unknown force in the universe that propels us forward.

Mark Twain provided another answer: He said the secret of success was to be able to make your vocation your vacation. When you love something and you are passionate about it, discipline comes easy.

Searching for—and Finding—What Makes You Happy

One day, a millionaire businessman took his son to the country to show him how the poor folks lived. They spent a few days on a farm with an extremely poor family that didn't have a fancy car, or a big extravagant home, or even the extra money to be able to go out to dinner now and then. After they returned home, the father asked his son what he thought of his experience.

"It was great, Dad," the son replied.

"Did you see how poor some people in this world are?" the father asked.

"I sure did. I saw that we have a dog, and they have four. We have a big pool in our backyard and they have a lake and a stream running through theirs that has no end. In our garden, we have fancy imported Italian oil lamps, and they have a sky filled with the stars. Our patio reaches all around to our front porch, and they have the entire horizon.

Thank you, Dad, for showing me how poor we really are."

What a great lesson for all of us. Life is totally a matter of perspective, and this boy hit it right on the head!

Some peoples' perspective is that their value as a human being comes from working long hours, driving big expensive SUV's, and making lots of money.

Me, I'm more of a BBQ on the back deck, guitar in the corner, hang out at the beach, playing with my kids type of guy. That's not to say that I don't enjoy the finer things in life, which I definitely do—but we all need to stick to our core values and beliefs.

CHAPTER 3

What Keeps Us From Being Passionate?

First, let's address some obstacles to the passionate life. Procrastination is a biggie. "I'll get to it tomorrow," "I'll take the kids to the park NEXT weekend," "I'll make that trip to Alaska when I retire," and "I'll buy that big TV I've been looking at for the last two years as soon as the old one breaks down." Well, what if that day never comes?

"Maybe when I'm older," "maybe when I'm more settled in my job," "maybe when the kids are out of the house." Procrastination is the great robber of time if you are not careful.

Nothing will suck the vigor for life faster than a good case of procrastination. Show me a desk that has papers piled high, or a garage stuffed with boxes and "I'll get to it later" projects, and I will show you a life that is not reaching its full potential. Nothing will stop a dream faster than when we ourselves stand in the way.

We put off organizing our desk, or exercising, or visiting a sick friend, or cleaning the garage, and so on . . . Well today *is* the first day of the rest of your life and it *does* matter! You can begin today to take control of your life and get back to that feeling of relevance!

I would say the most common killer of our motivation and passion is procrastination. It's caused by our perception that doing a certain task will cause us some sort of pain, and this is very important for all of us to realize at this point. Against that perceived pain, we must balance the enormous benefits.

Here's a piece of anonymous wisdom about procrastination:

> "They were going to be all that they wanted to be . . . tomorrow.
>
> None would be braver or kinder than they . . . tomorrow.
>
> A friend who was troubled and weary, they knew, would be glad of a lift—and needed it too. On him they would call—see what they could do . . . tomorrow.
>
> Each morning they stacked up the letters they'd write . . . tomorrow.
>
> The greatest of people they just might have been, the world would have opened its heart to them. But, in fact, they passed on and faded from view, and all that they left when their living was through was a mountain of things they intended to do . . . tomorrow."

I can't impress upon you enough to take action today, not tomorrow. If you can't see yourself realizing the dream, you never will. Just when you are about ready to succeed, something will pull you back. If you feel overwhelmed, break it down.

Just like eating an elephant, you can't eat it all at once, can you? Then break the big things in your life down into small, manageable tasks so you can eat it one bite at a time. And the longer you hold back, the harder it becomes. AH, but there's always tomorrow, right?

Limited ambitions are another obstacle to the passionate life. Dreams *should* be bigger than you; they should be a little bit out of reach, though not out of sight. Otherwise, they wouldn't be dreams, would they? When our dream exceeds our self image, I will promise you that as we get closer to our dream, we will very likely do something stupid to sabotage that dream . . . and keep ourselves from having that dream and realizing it.

Do what you love, dream big. Do it right or don't do it at all!

Pretend for a minute that when you wake up tomorrow, everything you do will be done to the best of your ability and you will give 110 percent effort to each and every activity that you had planned for your day. Do you think this would have much impact on how your day turned out? Absolutely! This would mean you couldn't take shortcuts, or do anything that was not done to the best of your ability.

I can remember when I was a freshman in high school and I had signed up for some sort of advanced math class. The teacher was also the head basketball coach, so there was good reason to do well in his class. Back in those days, I was doing three or four sports a year, and trying to excel at each was a challenge. For much of the first quarter, I did very well on all of the pop quizzes and exams that came my way.

Then, one day before practice, the coach said, "Mitche, I need you to come to my office tomorrow and retake a test." I asked why, and he replied that he thought that I may be cheating, since I never showed any of my work, only the answers, which were usually all correct. Since I was one of the stars of not only the basketball team, but also football and track, something like this could destroy any chance I had of earning an athletic scholarship to compete at the college level.

The next day, I showed up to his office to find a chalkboard full of equations and formulas, and about ten math problems. He then told me that I had sixty minutes to complete the exam. I looked at each problem, thought about it for a little while, did some basic calculations on the board, and then wrote down the final answer. It took me about 15 minutes to finish the test, and at the end I turned around and looked at the teacher, who had a big grin on his face.

"It appears that you like to take shortcuts and not show all of your work, Mr. Graf," which was indeed the case. I would do most of the work in my head, and then write down the correct answer without showing all of my work.

Since I did not show my work along the way, it was assumed that I must be cheating in some way since I simply wanted to get to the end game as fast as I could. After all, in track you are supposed to run as fast as you can—in a straight line!

Unfortunately, the rules in that math class did not allow for shortcuts, and neither does life, most of the time. A purpose-driven person knows when he or she can or can't take shortcuts—and realizes that the good things in life are usually a result of hard work, dedication, and the ability to play by the rules of the game. Shortcuts may or may not be permitted.

Being Resistant to Change

Another obstacle that prevents us from being effective and holds us back is the *resistance to change.* We are all creatures of habit and we like to be comfortable with our routines. Change is wonderful and exciting, as long as it's happening to someone else, right?

The Passionate Life

Since our life is in a constant state of flux, we have a tendency to gravitate towards our comfort zone. It's the place where most people perform the best. Comfort zones are neither good nor bad; it's just that we are creatures of habit and will always gravitate towards what we feel to be safe.

If you keep doing what you have always done, you will keep getting what you have always gotten. Here's the problem with comfort zones: Being good can keep us from being *great*!

And it's easy to do. We live in a world of autopilot . . . cooking, driving, texting, eating. Our subconscious mind takes over and we aren't even aware of what we are doing. Have you ever driven down the road and began thinking about that project at work that you really need to focus on, or you answer a call on your cell and get into a five-minute conversation—Then all of a sudden, you realize that you've gone five miles down the road without even being aware that you were driving? Our brain is a miraculous thing!

Lack of Discipline

Lack of discipline is another obstacle, and also prevents you from being passionate. Take an inventory of your life, your goals, aspirations, and visions for your future, finances, retirement, and your hobbies. If you show me a successful business person, I will show you someone who is disciplined and dedicated to their mission.

When I was in high school, I competed in the 400 meters at the Junior Olympics and did very well on a national level for several years. Between my coach, my parents, my friends (and my competition), I was able to create a very strong set of goals that I wanted to accomplish with my running. At one point, my times were on track to qualify for the U.S. Olympic Trials in Eugene, Oregon, but unfortunately, a torn hamstring ended my sprinting career in college, and I was forced to retire long before I was ready.

But there has been a lifelong impact. Athletics is a wonderful teacher of what setting goals can help you accomplish, and I believe that many of my core values and beliefs are rooted in the training I received from competing in sports.

Are you someone who gets up every day and waits to see how they feel before making any plans? Are you easily side-tracked or do you have a sense of purpose with an ability to stick to your plan? It's not that difficult to be dedicated if it's something you love and are passionate about.

Any discipline you desire must be built up gradually. If your goal is to run a marathon next year, you don't start out by running twenty-six miles on your first day of training, do you? You start with baby steps and work up from there.

When Mark Twain advised making your vocation a vacation, he knew that when you love what you are doing, whether your job or not, it's easy to be dedicated and disciplined.

So there you have a few of the obstacles to living the passionate life. Now let's talk more positively about what it means to you.

CHAPTER 4

What I Offer You—the Passionate Life

I want to drill deep into your mind and paint a portrait of the difference between simply plodding through life and serving time . . . and the passionate pursuit of life. My goal is to shake up your routine a little and give you a new sense of what's really important, what your purpose is . . . to give you a more fulfilling sense of passion for everything you do.

Whatever job you do for a living is not who you are; it's only what you do. You should take more pride in being a parent, a spouse, a friend. In all of these areas, you can be passionate.

So how do you live the passionate life? Well, you'll need to make some decisions along the way, and your entire approach to life may need to have a bit of an overhaul. Your attitude and how you allocate your time may also need to change. Over time, you will then slowly begin to wake up with a fire in your belly!

And you'll have to learn to see life's journey as a wonderful roller coaster ride filled with highs and lows, ebbs and flows, and total exuberance . . . and, of course, heartache.

This is My Moment!

When you are able to say those words, you will feel the birth of passion within yourself. You and I can surrender to the circumstances in our life that always seem to come our way from day to day, and live the "maintenance life," or we can tap into our deepest sense of purpose so that the circumstances won't matter.

Missed Moments and Self-Created Prisons

Through all of my experiences, good and bad, I have come to this conclusion about the human spirit: We could probably all write a novel about opportunities that have come our way and we did absolutely nothing about them. We saw the opportunity, but froze up under the pressure of "What if it doesn't work out?" "What if I fail?" "What if I make a fool of myself?"

Before long, we end up in a self-created prison that affects our entire life—our family, our emotions, our physical and financial health. We get so caught up in our circumstances that we forget about our life.

Let's say you get hit with some sort of bad luck, which is like a prison because it limits your options. It's real and it happens to you. A bad day at work, a bad week, a bad month, an argument with a friend or your spouse, some sort of financial dilemma, a bad year! The bad thing actually happens, and instead of dealing with it and moving on, we choose to let it bubble and fester, and we suppress it to the point that the world knows nothing about our situation. We get resentful that anything had the nerve to happen to us.

The Passionate Life

It's just not fair; it wasn't in your game plan. Have you ever had this experience before? Things that have happened, have happened. Life is sometimes fair and sometimes not. Unless the past affects you in some profound way, it's time to say, "It's water over the dam" and move on with your life.

Pain, Passion, and Meaning

One of my favorite artists of all time is Billy McLaughlin, who makes the most fascinating sounds come out of an acoustic guitar. Through the 80's and 90's, he was one of the best guitar players in the world and would play music that was like angels coming down from the heavens. He had devoted his life to his music.

In 1999, Billy began losing control on stage, and at first it was written off to having had a bad night or playing a few bad notes.

In 2001, he was diagnosed with Focal Distonia, an incurable neurological disorder. Years of dedication to his craft began to slip away. He continued to try with all his might and he kept trying, but there came a day when he was forced to quit.

By 2002, his career was over and his music was silenced. I can remember crying when I heard the news that he was done creating music. Coming to terms with the diagnosis of Distonia was a monumental change for Billy, and his outlook on life and what he was going to do without his passion changed him forever.

Then, in 2006, rumors surfaced that Billy was attempting a comeback. Billy had been relearning his music, one note at a time. He had been doing the impossible. He had been teaching himself to play all over again, note for note—LEFT HANDED!

The Passionate Life

It's not like walking backwards down the street or driving a British automobile. It's like learning to speak every word in reverse, phonetically! Focal Distonia took away Billy Mac's life as a musician, until his passion took it back!

I'm happy to say that he is once again inspiring audiences with his unique style of music and his passion lives on—left handed! I have met many passionate people in my life, but none hold a candle to the zest and zeal of Billy Mac!

Now *that* is passion! It's the kind of passion that I want to give you. I want to give you a shot of adrenaline into your soul so that you live a life of passion, whatever your life consists of.

I believe life is meant to be enjoyed to the fullest. It doesn't mean we won't have pain or heartache or face many obstacles. It's supposed to be something that at the end we say, "I had a good life"—and my Dash had meaning.

Passion About EVERYTHING

Purpose and motivation don't strike us like lightning. They have to be cultivated through practice. But life without them is a life not fulfilled to its full potential.

I'm here to tell you that the passion I'm talking about—the exuberant enthusiasm that seeps from your pores—is not a feeling that comes and goes, or a mood you wait to have in order to act on something. The passion I'm talking about is the way you approach your entire life, everything you do, every thought you think, *everything.*

A while back, I went on a scuba diving trip to Honduras with a bunch of people from all over the United States. As we all unpacked and got ready for our week in paradise, out came the fancy underwater cameras, the PDA devices for email, laptop computers, our expensive cigars, and all sorts of other amenities to help make our experience more enjoyable. Toys that we are all used to in our modern world and without them we almost feel naked!

As I ventured out into the town, I saw young children playing with empty cans in the street kicking them back and forth, back and forth. I saw people on their way to work, riding bikes and scooters instead of driving cars. I saw women hanging out the family laundry on clothes lines in their front yard. I saw the men cleaning the day's catch from the sea so they could take the meat home to feed their families.

I saw a side of humanity that we in the United States rarely get a chance to see. Most of us make as much money in a week as they make in an entire year, and their standard of living is not even close to being on the same level as ours.

But I also saw something else. I saw smiles on all their faces, and heard laughter coming from their houses, and saw people helping other people. And it all was being done at a much slower pace than I was used to. They didn't have any of the toys we all had, but they were happy! They also didn't have any of the stress that we live with on a daily basis. They were content with what they had, even if they didn't know there was something more out there. But at what cost? All they knew is what they had, and all they had is all that they knew. Nothing more. The simple things in life that we take for granted were cherished and held dear by the Hondurans.

We need to slow down, enjoy the journey, and not be in such a rush to get to wherever it is we are going. There are plenty of treasures along the way. If I could have bottled that spirit and brought it back with me, I would have done so in a heartbeat!

The Passionate Life

It's easy to forget about the little things that make us happy . . . holding a baby, going for a walk, watching a good sitcom or movie, getting a letter from a good friend, or even something as simple as watching the sunset on a warm evening.

Those are some of the facets of the passionate life that we were meant to live. The human heart was made for passion, for strong desire to reach for something beyond ourselves. We need to be able to celebrate each and every day of our lives, no matter the circumstances. We are born, we live, and we die. All we can control is the way we live.

CHAPTER 5

Passion as the Fuel for Our Journey

How far will our life's journey take us? That depends on how much of the right fuel you put into your tank . . . and passion is the fuel that's going to get you to your destination. The more right fuel you have for your life, the more fulfilled and rewarding your life is going to be.

Passion as a Permanent State of Mind

We all have moments of activity that give us some sort of temporary feeling of enthusiasm . . . a vacation, dinner with friends, watching your team win a game, or even a single déjà vu moment in the middle of the day when you seem to connect with yourself because of something that is said, or something that happens . . . your mind goes back to a place and time when you felt more alive and vibrant and had a strong sense of purpose.

But then it goes away and we are left with that feeling of incompletion. Our routine, or rut, wins out and we go back to what is comfortable and secure.

When most people think about bursts of emotion that come and go, they see passion as something that is mostly unnecessary to get through life and have the attitude, "Let's not get all worked up over something small. Let's just take it one day at a time and see where it takes us."

These folks are mired in *Passionatelessness.* They basically are robots, wandering the streets of life without any direction or conviction . . . no emotion, no fulfillment, and definitely no passion!

Do you ever get frustrated with your life or feel that your life has been taken over by routine instead of desire? Just to keep the car headed straight down the road . . . bills to pay, fences to fix, kids to get off to school, and you feel like you are just standing still instead of moving forward.

We get up, we go to work, we take care of the kids, we go to the store, we come home, we go to bed and then we start the whole process all over again tomorrow. We are losing both our passion and our purpose, and we are passing that lack of enthusiasm on to our kids. Sure, maybe a trip to the coast or a bonus from work might wake us out of our slumber for a little while, but pretty soon we are back to having no real enthusiasm about our life.

Do you feel like your day is filled with activities that are basically unproductive and worthless? Do you feel that your life is controlled by outside forces and you have no say in the matter? Are you satisfied with your life?

Sometimes it feels like you are simply treading water . . . getting through the end of the work day, or maybe just through your morning break, or to the 8:00 movie at the theater, to finish weeding the garden, or maybe something as simple as the motivation to get up and get yourself another cup of coffee!

When we are going through difficult times of our life, like the death of a family member, divorce, or perhaps the loss of a job, we may have a hard time getting motivated about doing *anything*! But if we can cultivate passion as the fuel for our journey, our level of passion will determine how far we go.

One Baby Step at a Time

That's because the passionate life isn't just one thing. Life is made up of a series of small tasks, and how we take—and take on—those baby steps will determine the quality of our life.

You can't eat the whole pie all at once! I have tried many a times in my life, but I always ended up feeling the same way—overstuffed, bloated and wishing I had eaten only one slice!

In other words, the answer to our problems is not always a deep, hidden thing that takes months of counseling to reveal. Sometimes a very simple and minor adjustment can bring tremendous change. It could be as small as making a decision to let go of the past, or getting more balance in your life, laughing more, doing more for others, or choosing more positive and uplifting friends.

One thing is certain: Nothing ever changes unless we make a decision and take some action. Don't forget to do little things that potentially have big power. So often, when we think of passion and drive, we think of big undertakings and wonder how in the world we will accomplish them. But little things can be just as effective, if not more powerful. A hug or a smile can change someone's day, or even maybe an entire life!

Passion as a Way of Life

If you like cheese as much as I do, then you probably have had the opportunity sometime in your life to visit a factory where they make cheese. One of my favorite places is the Tillamook Cheese Factory in Tillamook, Oregon. You walk in and are immediately overcome by the immensity and grandness of the building. If you choose, you can get a guided tour behind the scenes and hear about the entire process from beginning to end. If you know anything about making cheese, you know it all starts with milk from a cow, and if you have ever been to Tillamook, Oregon, you know there are cows everywhere!

Exact ingredients, temperatures, and aging are combined to give each type of cheese its distinctive flavor and texture. There are conveyer belts, and cheese cutters, and quality control personnel making sure that every single block of cheese meets rigorous standards; there are wrappers, boxers, stackers and loaders. The big boxes are loaded onto a big truck and then carried away to the retail stores, where you and I can go in, buy the block of cheese and take it home where it can be enjoyed!

They definitely have their system down, and if anywhere along the way, a part of the system fails, the cheese doesn't make it to our refrigerator and then into our bellies.

Every step along the way is controlled by a process, so that at the end of that process, a marvelous block of cheese is produced that tastes exactly like the block of cheese you bought last week at the store.

Just like in the making of a good block of cheese, the way you approach your life should be organized into a process or a system as well.

Passion is much more than just an emotion; it's an entire philosophy of life and how you live it. From beginning to end....Alpha to Omega.

CHAPTER 6

Busy-Ness and Focus, Sharpening the Axe

Everyone today seems busy. Ask just about anyone how they are, and they will probably respond with something like, "Man, it's seems that I'm busier than ever these days!" We are making a huge mistake if we equate being busy with being successful.

Once upon a time, there was a very big and strong woodcutter that got a job working for a local business. The pay was great and he got all the typical benefits. Because he was so excited about his pay and benefits, the woodcutter was determined to do his absolute best. He wanted to be a success at his new job and impress the boss. His boss gave him an axe and showed him the area where he was to work.

The Passionate Life

The first day the woodcutter brought back twenty-five trees. "That's great," said the boss. "Keep up the good work!"

Very motivated by the boss's words, the woodcutter tried even harder the second day, but he could only bring back fifteen trees. The third day, no matter how hard he tried, he only brought back ten trees. Day after day, no matter how much effort and energy he gave, he kept bringing back fewer and fewer trees.

"Something must be wrong with me, I'm losing my strength," the woodcutter surmised. He went to the boss and apologized, saying he could not understand what was going on.

"When was the last time you sharpened your axe?" asked the boss.

"Sharpen? I didn't have time to sharpen my axe. I have been too busy cutting trees!"

Are you polishing and adding to your skills, instead of doing the same thing over and over, year after year? When was the last time you really learned anything new? Have you been just cutting trees instead of sharpening the axe?

In the passionate life, the equivalent of sharpening the axe is sharpening your focus.

The Problem

It is not an easy task, I admit. We live in the digital age, where thousands of messages are sent to us every day. We are overloaded with information. The amount of leisure time enjoyed by the average U.S. citizen has decreased by about 35 percent since the early 70's. All these gadgets like cell phones, laptop computers, iPhones, Blackberries, PDAs, PSPs, Wii's, and GPSs have sucked our personal time right out from underneath us . . . it can drive you nuts!

Perhaps if we did less, we could do more things with excellence. Part of our problem in the world is most people are trying to do so much that they can't do any of it right. Slow down, think about what you are doing, and ask yourself if you are doing any of it with your whole heart.

Choosing to focus

Is there anything you love enough to dedicate your entire being to? In order to love what you do, you must do what you love. I believe that when we are passionate about the right things, the activity required to accomplish those things will energize us. That doesn't mean we don't get tired, but rather our tiredness is a satisfying, fulfilling type of tired.

When you choose to stay focused, you may have to cut some things out of your life that you enjoy—but are not bearing fruit. There are a lot of things in life that are good in some way, but they may not be good things for you!

For example, I have spent the better part of the last twelve years in the professional photography industry, and during that time, there have been some major changes; the biggest was digital photography. As a whole, the digital revolution has been the best thing ever to come along for professional photographers, as well as the worst.

It seems like everybody and their brother's friend's aunt's sister is now a "photographer," which has put a crunch on the true professionals. The "Weekend Warriors" and "Soccer Moms" have taken the industry by storm with their $500 cameras.

What has happened with many professional photographers is that they have become slaves to their computers and their workflow. Things that used to be handled by the professional color labs are now being dealt with by the photographers themselves, thus adding a significant number of hours to their already-long work week.

In photography, only three things make you money: shooting, selling, and marketing. Retouching a digital file doesn't fall under any of those categories, but many pros are being consumed by this digital process.

It doesn't bother us to cut things out of our lives that we dread and despise anyway, but what if the thing we need to cut off is something to which we are attached? That makes it a lot harder, because our emotions are involved. Photographers that spend eight hours on a Sunday editing and retouching all the files from the wedding they photographed on Saturday are attached to an outdated method of performing their work. Instead of hiring the job out to someone so they could free up a substantial amount of time, they choose to do it themselves because they are emotionally attached to the digital process. Doing $10-$15 per hour work is not what business owners should be doing with their time, whatever industry they are in!

Sharpening focus means knowing what you want out of life. I don't just mean goals for your business. What is it you want out of your life personally? Time with your family, time to travel if that's what you enjoy, time for your gardening or reading, or other hobbies and passions you may have . . . or listening to some really good music, watching old movies, wetting a fishing line, taking in an art show, ready the funny papers, golfing, or other hobbies and passions you may have. Most importantly, what about time for yourself?

Think about these important questions:

- ❖ How many days off a week do you want?

- ❖ What will you do with your free time?

- ❖ Where would you like to travel?

- ❖ What hobbies would you like to spend more time on?

- ❖ What kind of car do you want to drive?

The Passionate Life

- ❖ What kinds of clothes do you want to wear?

- ❖ What kind of house do you want to live in?

- ❖ Which relationships are most important to you, and how can you nurture them?

- ❖ How much money is it going to take to support this lifestyle?

Then you have the professional goals:

- ❖ How many hours per week are you going to work?

- ❖ How are you going to progress up the ladder at work so you can make more money and take on more responsibility?

- ❖ How can you improve as a worker, boss, owner, etc., so that you can make the money you need to support your lifestyle choices?

Deciding what you want is the all-important first step towards getting it.

Success and the Power of the Mind

Here's another point on the power of words. Success takes both physical stamina—low energy people are rarely successful—and mental acuteness. In particular, it requires the ability to visualize.

Let's do an exercise that shows the power of your mind. Imagine there's a lemon sitting on the table in front of you right now . . . grab a knife, and cut it into wedges. You can smell the aroma radiating off the lemon as it fills the air with its fragrant smell. Take a wedge right now, in your mind's eye, and take a bite.

Are you salivating at all? That's the power of words. Words are simply tools that allow you to create a dream, that vision of where you want to be in your life.

Do you have a vision of your dream embedded in your brain so that it's so compelling that it drives you to where you need to be? Is it as compelling as the lemon?

We have been taught to believe that our dreams are not meant to come true, and that dreaming takes us away from the task at hand, which is just to get through today. People who are accused of being daydreamers are said to be lazy, or foolish, or even "not plugged into reality." Yet . . . how does anything get done if it is not imagined beforehand?

Daydreaming, despite its negative reputation, is the final key to sharpening your focus on what you really want. Every invention known to mankind, and every great idea, was birthed at one time by someone who "daydreamed." I have been accused of being a daydreamer for much of my life, but I can honestly say that many of my "bright ideas" have been the result of my mind being allowed to wander around for awhile.

Once upon a time, there was a caveman who daydreamed about making fire, but it took us over one million years for us to figure out how to utilize it. Did you know that some daydreamed about inventing ice cream over 2000 years BC, but it wasn't until only 100 years ago someone came up with the idea for . . . the ice cream cone. In 1775 . . . the flush toilet. In 1857—82 years later—toilet paper!

Our entire world is filled with the results of daydreamers who believed that they could make the world a better place.

CHAPTER 7

Taking Responsibility

Passionate people are engaged with life. They take responsibility. It's easy to try to blame someone else for our bad decisions or lack of success, when in reality it's nobody's fault but our own.

We all have had times when life didn't seem to play very fair, and we felt like the world was out to get us. I can remember times in my own life when it seemed that everything I was doing didn't turn out as I had planned. I felt as if I were doing the right things with the right amount of effort, but the dice just didn't roll my way.

Looking back at all of my failures, whether in business, relationships, or life's situations, I can say with 110 percent certainty that the reason I failed was because of *my* attitude and *my* effort.

Also, it's not your potential that is the issue. You will lose with potential alone, but you win with effectiveness. How many times have you heard in your life, "Oh, you have so much potential." You can die from a terminal case of potential!

Attitude Ignites Passion

Taking responsibility is a matter of attitude, which is the match that sets passion afire. We can decide to have a better attitude in life so that passion can arise. A bad attitude can kill passion.

Lazy people with bad attitudes are always unhappy, and they can't understand why. Do you know anyone like that? Maybe they spend too much time talking about all the cool TV shows they watch every day, or spend all their time keeping up with everyone else's business.

To live passionately, you must avoid becoming stagnant and inactive and developing a terminal case of "bad attitude." If you have lost the joy in your journey, maybe it's because you have allowed a bad attitude to creep into your soul. We must take responsibility for that.

To me, "attitude" is much more important than your past, or education, or money, or circumstances, or failures, or successes, or what other people think, say, or do. It's more important than appearance or skill. If all but one of the strings on our guitar are broken, then all we can do is play on the one string we have left, and that is our attitude. I am convinced that life is 5 percent what happens to me, and 95 percent how I react to it.

In an earlier chapter, I mentioned the importance in taking responsibility: keeping yourself stimulated and enriched.

The Passionate Life

It's very easy for us to fall into that old management trap and get caught up in the day-to-day details of managing our business. We end up running our business instead of designing our lives. You know what I mean. Answering phones, managing the personnel, ordering supplies, keeping up with the marketing and promotion, cleaning the bathroom, mowing the lawn, doing the books...and on and on. Before we know it, we are working seven days a week, sixteen hours a day, week after week, month after month. Friday nights, Sunday mornings, holidays. And for what?

We don't even have time for our families. We don't have time to play with our children, or to drop a fishing line in the water, or hit that golf ball up and down the fairway, or watch our favorite show on the weekend. The things that are most important to us start slowly slipping away, and we become a slave to our business rather than its master.

No matter how enthusiastic you are, you will become stagnant if you don't take responsibility for keeping yourself stirred up. You can get stagnant with your job, your marriage, and your relationships with friends, your hobbies, and your life! Anything not moving is on its way to becoming stagnant and boring, which is definitely what we want to avoid if we are talking about truly embracing our lives with passion and purpose.

If you are bored with yourself, try a different look or a new hair color. Eat at a new restaurant, take a short trip to the new mall and get some different clothes, or go do something you have never done before. Take a risk! You might like it, and then again, you might not. But you will *never* know unless you try.

Again, it is *you* who is responsible for making the decision to act. If you step up to the plate, you might strike out, but if you don't try, you will never know the true joy of hitting a home run. Barry Bonds has struck out more than anyone in the history of baseball, but he has also hit more home runs than anybody in history as well. It's when we take a risk or face a fear that we move forward in our lives.

Private Time

Often we are our own best advisors. We need a relationship with ourselves, so that we can spend quiet time with nobody around but us, and enjoy it.

When I get bored and in search of answers or want to jolt my life a little, I go to the mountains in Montana. The simple things like building a campfire, listening to the sounds of Mother Nature, watching the morning mist rise from the wet grass and river, getting up before dawn and sneaking outside to build a campfire with a good cup of coffee or something hot . . . nothing gets more basic than that!

It's almost like Mother Nature is the battery for my soul and I can easily get in touch with myself very quickly when she's around. Regardless of what is going on in life, she always seems to put things back into their place and this gives me proper perspective.

What happens when you take responsibility, have a purpose in life, and are determined to live life to its fullest?

It was over 50 years ago that a big dreamer named Walt Disney sat down with a group of very intelligent businessmen and began to paint a picture and describe a vision that he had—to build the biggest and the best theme park in the world! And as he began to describe his vision of a place he called Disneyland, he said that he also already knew the man who he wanted to oversee the project. "I don't know his name, but I know who he is. I want you to go out and find the man who put the United

States Navy back in the Pacific Ocean after Pearl Harbor was bombed.

His staff went around the country trying to find this man who was to be the leader of Walt Disney's grand vision. They finally came up with the man's name. His name was Admiral Joe Fowler. Joe came to Walt Disney's office and sat down and began to listen as Walt painted a picture of his vision for a theme park where families could go and enjoy themselves together. Joe Fowler laughed and said, "Do you understand who I am? I just won World War II and you want me to work for a guy who draws cartoons for a living?" Walt wouldn't take no for an answer even though Joe kept saying, "I'm retired. I'm done working."

Finally, Walt's persistence paid off and Admiral Joe Fowler began to see his dream. At the young age of 56, Joe Fowler started an entirely new career and oversaw the building of Disneyland.

You may think that's the end, but it's only the beginning! Many years later, Walt Disney approached Joe again and said, "I want to build Disney World. Once again his clear vision was so compelling that at the age of 77, Joe Fowler built Disney World.

Then, 10 years later at the ripe old age of 87, Walt Disney wanted to build Epcot Center, so once again he approached Admiral Joe Fowler. By the end of this, Joe's attitude had changed just a little bit. Instead of saying, "I'm done. I'm retired, I'm finished," he said, "You don't have to die until you want to."

There's a message there for all of us! Joe had no idea when his time would be up, but he took responsibility for living every minute of it to the fullest.

The Passionate Life

Passion and Entrepreneurship

One of the consequences of taking responsibility is that you can wind up linking your life to a purpose. We all have a reservoir of passion welled up inside of us; it's just a matter if finding how to turn on the spigot.

So, what is usually the number one reason for starting your own business? Is it the joy of being a self-employed entrepreneur and being able to dictate your own hours? Is it the money? Is it the ability to dream your own dreams and reach for the stars? Is it the ability to breathe life into your own business creation and watch as it becomes successful and profitable over time?

Actually, these are all reasons many people today are putting everything on the line and starting their own business, but the main reason is that we have a passion for what we do! The gardener who starts a nursery, the weekend BBQer who opens a restaurant, the woodworker who starts a cabinet shop, or the photographer who decides to open a studio. We all share a common passion for what we do.

If you are a business owner, you hopefully are full of this passion and desire to become the best you possibly can be.

CHAPTER 8

The Importance of Humor: Lighten Up!

The passionate person knows how to maintain a balanced life. Take your job seriously—but yourself lightly. It's called having a sense of humor! If we can figure out a way to keep it light in the face of stress and change, we will be healthier, happier, and above all, have a more fulfilling feeling about ourselves!

Did you know stress is the number one killer in the United States? When things get difficult in our life, we get overwhelmed with that feeling of uneasiness. Most stress is caused by change, and our world is overflowing with change everyday!

Having a sense of humor is not something that you are born with. It is a set of developed skills that allows us to keep flexible in the face of stress and change, and it really has nothing to do with joke telling, even though most people associate it with telling a joke. Do you think you can tell a good joke? More than likely, you don't. Actually, only about 2 percent of the population can remember punch lines and tell a good joke.

Having a sense of humor is something else altogether. Do you feel you have a good sense of humor? There are humorless people in this wonderful world of ours that go through life with a case of terminal professionalism. You know the type: "If I'm going to be successful, I must be hard driving, hard headed, I must be serious. I don't have time to be laughing and playing around. Leave me alone. I'm having a really good bad day!"

Those are the kinds of people who end up with nervous breakdowns, premature deaths, or worse yet, as old, bitter, and crotchety neighbors! We need to smile and get enjoyment from the simple things in life—a newborn baby, a sunny day, a great new recipe, a flower popping through the ground in early spring, a great drive off the tee!

Having a sense of humor won't solve any of the world's problems, but it sure makes it easier to get us through those tough days that pop up every now and then. It has the magical ability to sustain life.

I've noticed that when people are on their deathbeds, they don't say they wished they owned more toys, or had more money. They say things like, "I wish I'd worked less and played more."

Benefits of Laughter

The effect of laughter on your body is immediate and amazing. When you laugh until your sides hurt, your cheeks ache, you have tears in your eyes, and you almost pee your pants, the process actually lowers your blood pressure, reduces stress hormones, and increases muscle flexion. Plus, it increases your resistance to infections and other types of diseases. After a good laugh, we have that feeling of being cleansed from head to toe, and our souls are refreshed. In fact, if it's a really good laugh, the smile may last all day!

Laughter triggers the release of endorphins, which is a pain killer produced by your brain. Laughing gives you the same sensation that marathon runners report feeling at the 18-20 mile mark, better known as "hitting the wall."

They will tell you that just when they think they can't stand any more pain and want to drop out of the race, their bodies give them a little special treat in the form of endorphins. A sense of euphoria and peace usually accompanies their other feelings and they can then push through to the end of the race. It's almost as if their bodies know they are about to go through some excruciating pain and will release the endorphins to help them deal with it.

I don't know about you, but I would much rather spend time laughing every day instead of running a marathon to get that feeling of happiness!

I'm attracted to happy people, for the selfish reason that they put me in a better mood. Happiness is contagious. It spreads like the flu. When one person is happy, the mood tends to spread to others!

Progress, Stress and Change

Part of the reason we find it difficult to keep it light is that the world we live in is full of stress! Stress isn't something new to mankind, since most of our history is overflowing with change, which is what causes stress.

But today, progress itself has vastly increased the stressors, both actual and potential, in our lives. Did you know that before 1965, 85 percent of all knowledge didn't even exist? In the past ten years, there have been 1,000,000 new commercials on TV, 20,000 new shopping malls, the Internet as we know it, and cell phones that can act as entertainment centers.

No wonder we have such a difficult time keeping it light in the face of such radical changes in our world. But it's all a matter of perspective, as our thoughts can either keep us healthy or make us ill. It's all up to us. Being adaptable is one of the best traits you can have.

Keeping Perspective

There is a wonderful place I like to go to in Mexico called Pamuul. It's in the middle of nowhere, and all it has is a bunch of bungalows, a restaurant, and a dive shop. That's it! No stores, no traffic, no people! It's the perfect place to get away from it all and let your batteries be recharged.

The bungalows are only about 100 feet away from the Caribbean Ocean, there's a hammock in front of the private porch, and the water is some of the clearest in the entire world! If all of my businesses weren't in the United States, I would probably spend at least six months a year down there. It's as close to heaven on earth as you can get, in my opinion. In fact, they even have Wi-Fi in the rooms!

My wife, Tami, on the other hand, looks at the accommodations with a different set of eyes. It's too far away from civilization, the bungalows are old and squeaky, you can smell the salt water mold and mildew at night when you sleep, and there are all sorts of little critters that fly around at night!

I have worked on her over the years and she now admits that she *may* be willing to spend a couple of months down there each year with our kids, so perhaps Pamuul is beginning to grow on her (just like the mold inside the bungalows!). Same reality—different perspectives. What can be one person's heaven can be another person's nightmare! We are all hard-wired with a set of innate perspectives on how we view the world.

Those wires are difficult to rewire, but they can be changed if given the right tools and the right fuel.

Another way to keep your sense of humor is to remember that being successful has nothing to do with how much money you make or how many hours you work at the office. It's all about proper balance in your life. We all need to be reminded from time to time that life is very short, fragile, and precious.

I'm always reminding myself to lighten up. My job is only a job. Success is a constantly evolving journey, not merely a destination. To set your sights on the future, you must have a vision of where you want to go. After all, we drive with our focus in the distance, not on the highway as it passes beneath us. My favorite story on this point comes from Lewis Carroll. As Alice was walking through Wonderland, she came to a fork in the road and met the Cheshire cat. Alice said, "Which road do I take?" And the Cheshire cat said, "Well, where do you want to go? Alice responded, "I don't know." And the Cheshire cat said, "Then any road will get you there."

Success is not a destination. If you are not happy with where you are, you won't be happy with where you are going either. It's all an inside job!

CHAPTER 9

Goals and the Power of the Dream

Psychologists say that we spend 90 percent of our time thinking about ourselves, specifically, our past and our present. Isn't that amazing? This leaves us little time to think about the future. *The magic lies in your future and in your future thinking!* You must have a dream or a set of dreams that are so compelling, that even when life knocks you down, you keep your eyes on the prize at the end of the tunnel.

The only thing that keeps us moving forward is having enough value in the vision of our future so that we can move us from our present state to where we want to be. That's the power of the dream. People with no direction or goals tend to frustrate me. I see a lot of wasted potential, and I know waste always leads to regret. I know people who have wasted their lives, and now they are old and have nothing but regret about what they didn't do.

So, what is your dream? The thoughts and ideas in your brain rule your world. When you have a dream, a passion, a goal, nothing can stop you! If you don't have a dream, a goal . . . You might as well be DEAD!

Potential, Passion, and Visualization

I'm going to tell you a story about a little girl, who was told by her gymnastics coach, of all people, to quit and do something else. "You're not fast enough, you can't jump high enough, and you're not strong enough!" She went to her Mom with huge tears in her eyes saying that she didn't want to quit because she loved gymnastics too much, but her mother encouraged her not to.

Several years later, this young girl was standing at the end of a ramp—and more eyes were on her at that moment in time than any athlete in the history of the world. All she needed to do was run down this ramp, hit the springboard, vault over a wooden horse, stick the landing, and in the process score a perfect 10.

She had many obstacles. First of all, this was the Olympic Games. Second, the Eastern European judges had never given American competitors favorable scores. Also, a short time before, she had completed her first jump, and it was the best score she had ever had in her life—a 9.86. To top it all off, six weeks earlier, she'd had knee surgery! That would be a huge obstacle for any of us.

Any one of those obstacles would have prevented most people from even starting. She needed a 10. *She got a 10*! This four-foot, eleven-inch fireball was Marylou Retton.

Do me a favor: Imagine that it's *you* standing at the end of the ramp and *you* have to run down, hit the ramp, and stick the landing . . . with the entire world watching you.

How do you feel? What obstacles are holding you back? What's keeping you from being successful in your life?

Don't you think that she practiced that jump thousands of times before in her mind? She was like the basketball player who visualizes shooting free throws. Do you think he sees himself missing the shots? Of course not. He makes every one!

Your mind can't tell the difference between a clearly visualized event in your mind and the real thing. If you tell yourself that it's going to be a great day, guess what? It usually turns out that way. On the other hand, if you wake up already thinking that the day is going to be in the toilet, guess what usually happens?

Our brain will believe whatever we tell it! Knowing this, why don't we wake up every day of our lives telling ourselves that today is going to be the best day of our life?

Hopes and Dreams

There's an innate desire deep inside each of us that wants to reach goals that may seem unreachable. Hopes and dreams that may have been slumbering around in the depths of our hearts that have been there for so long that they have cobwebs growing on them! But hope is what makes us human. Animals assume every day is going to be like the previous. They go through the seasons, instinctively acting out their preprogrammed behaviors. But humans hope and have dreams, integral components to the passionate life.

When we talk about embracing our purpose passionately, it is natural to talk about our dreams, because dreams help stir our passion just as passion helps stir our dreams. It's important to think big when it comes to dreams for our future. Too many of us don't think big enough, and I believe little thinkers will live little lives. People who cannot conceive of anything beyond what they can see with their eyes miss out on the best!

The Passionate Life

Hopes, dreams, and visions are like seeds. Though they are small at the beginning, they grow over time, perhaps into something truly impressive.

Living YOUR Life

So, we should get busy doing what we are good at or doing what *we* want to do, instead of what others are good at and what others want us to do. It's important to respect and to examine what you're really doing with your "dash time."

CHAPTER 10

What You Make of It

When a difficult challenge faces you, don't ask why; ask what you can learn from it that will make you into a better person. Be thankful that you have experienced the low valleys of life so that you can appreciate the mountain tops.

There are two kinds of people in the world, Optimists and Pessimists. Each is prone to certain habits or thought processes. Positive people tend to look at bad events or misfortune as being only temporary. They get better jobs, live longer, live better, and age better. Negative people tend to believe that bad events last a long time and will undermine everything, and they get depressed more easily. We all know people that are in each category, don't we? It's all about the self-talk, some of which is said out loud.

Optimistic people always seem to find a way to take advantage of a situation and not be burdened by it. They aren't lazy. They don't wait for opportunities to come to them; they go after the opportunity!

Common sense tells us that success breeds optimism. On the other hand, failure or lack of success makes it easier to look at the world with a pessimistic perspective. So what's the difference between someone who seems to always have a smile on their face and someone who always seems to be soured on everything? Chances are that one of those people has given up, and the other has not.

It's all in what you make of it. Consider the person who puts himself on a strict diet, then on Friday night goes out for dinner and a few drinks with some friends. He eats a little more than he should, drinks more than he should, then the next morning the negative self-talk begins: "I can't even go out to dinner without making a total fool out of myself. All my friends must think I'm a total loser. My diet is ruined forever. I might as well have really blown it and ordered that triple chocolate brownie."

Positive self-talk would sound more like, "Well, last night wasn't my best example of self-restraint, but it's only one night, and I was doing really well up until then. Today, I will refocus my commitment to my diet and get back on track."

It's all about what happens—and what we make of it. The little conversations we have with ourselves will determine the outcome of most situations we are faced with in our lives.

Any Day Can be a "10"

Several years ago, I received a phone call from my sister informing me that my stepfather had just died from a massive stroke. I flew out the following morning to be with my family and spent the better part of the week spending time with family and friends. At the young age of 49, with the best part of his life still ahead of him, he was taken from us in an instant.

We spent the week talking about the good times, remembering the laughter, and crying until we didn't have any more tears left. As the week went along, our emotions seemed to elevate to the point that we laughed louder and we cried bigger. When it was time for all of us to return to our lives, I can remember feeling like my entire spirit had just been cleansed, and I felt like I had a renewed sense of perspective on my own life.

I wouldn't trade that time for anything in the world. It's at those moments in life that you talk about things that you normally don't talk about. It made me realize that everyday *can* be a "10" day, for your family, friends, co-workers, employees, yourself. We should never let a day go by that we don't tell the people that mean the most to us that we love them. Life is much too short to *not* do it!

Realize that every day can be a 10. The past is history, the future is unknowable. All we have is right now. That's it. You absolutely never know what's going to happen—or what experiences lie around the corner.

Here's an example: Taking time off and unplugging my brain from the world is important to me, and I firmly believe in taking lots of time off to decompress from my work. When I have the choice, it's usually on a warm beach somewhere away from people, or in the mountains away from people. I make my living dealing with people, but when I'm not working, I want to disconnect from it all and immerse myself in solitude and spend time with my family.

One of our recent vacation spots was Kauai, Hawaii, where we spent ten days at a five-star resort eating outstanding food and playing for hours in the largest pool in Hawaii. In addition, the resort had well over 1000 rooms, six restaurants, and a mini shopping mall. So right from the start I knew it was going to be a different kind of experience for me! There was an activity department for kids, nightly entertainment in the lounge, and all sorts of other activities that you could choose to be involved in.

On the Friday before we came home, I noticed on the daily schedule of events that there was going to be a presentation from one of the locals on "How to Live on a Coconut." It sounded intriguing so we headed down to the room where the presentation was being held. When we walked in, there were only three other people in the room besides us, which seemed a bit strange, considering there were over 1000 rooms and probably 2000 people or more staying in the hotel.

I felt bad for this gentleman with only a small handful of people in his program, but he started on time and began to weave a beautiful story about all the wonderful things you can do with a coconut. You can make hats, plant holders, flutes, plates, decorations, wall art, and, of course, you can eat it! As he went along, you could almost feel his intensity increase as he showed us the techniques involved in cracking open a fresh coconut as to not spill the milk from inside.

I found myself fascinated by the knowledge that he possessed and didn't even realize that his 30-minute program had now become 90 minutes! He was so passionate about the coconut that time just melted away. That passion was transferred to the few people that were in the audience, and it's something that has stuck with me ever since.

At the end of his presentation, he told us about some of the items he made that he had for sale, and I felt obligated to purchase something from him. Most of the items were too big and bulky to take back home in the suitcase, so I ended up buying a Hawaiian "nose flute" that will only make noise when you blow air through your nose into the flute. For some reason, it sounded much better when he played it.

On most of my overseas trips, I like to bring a little souvenir home with me to remember where I'd been. Whether it be the famous "chicken man" from Mexico, or a talking bottle opener from England, or an Aboriginal boomerang from Australia, my wife always says, "That will look great in your office," which means it isn't going in the house! I can proudly say that my Hawaiian nose flute is proudly displayed right next to my Tribal mask from New Zealand—in my office!

You Decide

So you decide: Optimist or Pessimist? What you watch, the people you hang around with, and what you do—It all gets into your brain and is interpreted by your perspectives, thoughts, and beliefs.

You can decide whether you're an optimist or a pessimist. The way you think will direct the course of your life. If you say to yourself, I can't do that, it's too difficult, I don't have what it takes. Guess what? It *will* be too difficult, and you *won't* have what it takes. There is a very large likelihood that you will prove yourself right.

The old saying, "Man becomes what he dreams about all day long" is as true now as it ever was. Take ownership of that magnificent gift!

Changing Yourself Isn't Easy

If you have ever been involved with working with clay, you know that it's a very long and drawn-out process that requires patience. You begin the process with a big lump of clay that has no particular shape, purpose, or value. Over a period of about ten days that lump of clay will be worked, reworked, soaked, reworked again, trimmed, finished, fired, glazed, and re-fired. Once it's been fired, it becomes hardened so that the clay cannot be molded any further and the piece, in the form of an ashtray, a cereal bowl, or a coffee mug, will be able to withstand the elements and the rigors of life.

Even a beginner knows that in order to end up with something worthwhile, you have to know ahead of time what you are making! If you simply threw the lump of clay onto the potter's wheel without knowing what you wanted to make, chances are you would end up with a big lump of clay! You have to have an idea of what it is you are trying to accomplish before you begin the process of formation and transformation.

It's just like the caterpillar's calling to become a butterfly. It's meant to strain and grow and change—and the chrysalis or its cocoon is part of this process. Before it emerges from its sheltered cocoon and flies away, it must struggle and strain to get out so it can fulfill its destiny. It's a process. You are not meant to stay inside a cocoon forever, you are meant to fly.

CHAPTER 11

Taking Action

Success as a Journey

We all dream of different destinations. We say, "If I could only arrive, things would be just fine." *Not true!* It's all in the intermediate steps, including the early ones, that determine *how and when* you arrive.

In order to begin the race, it's very simple . . . *Start running!* Most people want to study the race, map it out, and diagram it; they want to lay out and design the race, they want to talk about the race, they want to read books about running the race . . . but they won't start running! Forget about waiting for the inspiration to suddenly hit you, just start running. As the Nike slogan says, JUST DO IT!

The Passionate Life

Action Ignites Motivation

Exercise, read a book, sign up for a class, organize your desk . . . and once you begin, the motivation will come and make it easier for you to keep on doing it!

How many people miss out on an experience in life because they wait until they *feel* motivated? They wait, and hope, and wait some more, and say things like, "Well, when I'm ready or when I know more, I will start." "When I have more money, or time, or when the snow melts, or when the kids are older." Blah, blah, blah, blah . . .

A key to running the race is to jump in there and start running. Things will *never* be perfect. Success comes to people who do today what they were thinking about doing tomorrow.

Goal setting is a great start, but goal "doing" is even better! Ninety percent of all goals are never achieved. At best, setting a goal is nothing but the beginning of the race.

Taking purposeful action: Excellence is a choice

Most people live in an ocean of mediocrity. "I guess good enough is good enough." If you are one of these people, there is nobody to blame but yourself. Excellence is a choice, just like attitude. We are mediocre *not* because of our background, our talent, the conditions, bad luck, or our personality. We are mediocre because we have *chosen* to be mediocre.

Rising above mediocrity is *never* an accident. It's always because of effort, and it has no finish line. Competitive excellence requires the decision to focus all of the time—not 50 percent, not 90 percent, but all of the time. Life without focus is like running a race without a finish line.

Grab your shoes and start running. Quit waiting for the perfect day because it will never come. The perfect salary, the perfect job, the perfect house, and the perfect environment are not prerequisites to rolling up your sleeves and getting to it!

The Energy to Take Action

Don't worry about having the energy if your dream truly energizes you. Nothing energizes us like having a clear vision of what we are suppose to be doing. We have to work in order to survive, but meaningless work wears us out! The world is filled with tired, worn-out people, most of them going through the motions of life, without finding their purpose. They spend their lives doing what they hate and are not courageous enough to do what they really want to do.

Sadly, one of the biggest motivators for people is often a paycheck. You would be better off to make less money and be passionate about what you are doing, than to make a lot of money doing something you despise!

Reasons for procrastination are endless: "Maybe when I'm older," "maybe when I'm more settled in my job," "maybe when the kids are out of the house," "maybe when I retire." Procrastination, as I mentioned earlier, is an obstacle to the passionate life, and it can rob you of time if you are not careful.

Passionate people avoid things that waste time. If we allow it, anything can become addictive. For example, have you ever spent an entire night looking for something good to watch on TV, and in the meantime you watch show after show of meaningless, mindless garbage? Not only can this be extremely taxing on your energy level, but it doesn't allow you to focus on the real issue, which is how to make *you* better. Most importantly, it doesn't free up your mind to allow the expansive thinking that separates "good" from "great."

The answer is planning ahead: developing that all-important mindfulness about how you're using your "dash time" makes all the difference. Be committed to *not* wasting any more of your time!

The Pointlessness of Complaining

One of the biggest time wasters is complaining. We can complain about the weather, about our job, about what we don't have, about the traffic, about our spouse or a co-worker, or about how bad the government is and that the whole world is out to get us, but complaining is a total waste of time. Nothing positive ever comes from it. It only creates a negative atmosphere where negativity begins to feed on itself and eventually fills life itself with misery.

Applying Knowledge

Another place where discipline is key is in applying knowledge. I don't care how much money you make or how many awards you have won, once you stop learning, it all just doesn't matter as much.

Knowledge is *not* power. It never has been, and it never will be. It's only applying that knowledge that becomes powerful. We all think we know it's better to be organized. But how many of us actually apply the lesson? Let me ask you: Do you think you know the value of being organized more than your desk, kitchen, or car would indicate? You see, it's not what you know; it's what you *do* with what you know that's important. On the same token, it's not what you have; it's what you *do* with what you have.

Looking for the Edge

Why are discipline, dedication, and action so important? Everyone is looking for the edge in life. Do you think that you are the only person in the world that's trying to find that little something that will make a big difference in their lives? Sometimes it's the smallest of differences that make the difference.

The Passionate Life

The Importance of Preparation

And it is disciplined practice that can make that difference. Have you ever trained for something strenuous, like running a race? What if you were to set out on the race without ever having worked out or developed your muscles? What if instead you sat around everyday eating all sorts of junk food and watching the tube? As much as your mind would want to work, once the race began, your body would let you down. We choose to practice doing what is right, and as we do it over and over, we form positive habits that become part of our inner fabric.

CHAPTER 12

Traits of the Ultra-Passionate

Now that I've described the passionate life in a general way, let me talk about the qualities of truly passionate people. It's been said that if you love what you do for a living and are passionate about it, you won't have to work a day in your life. Many of us experience small moments of triumph throughout our lives. At those times, we love what we are doing and are passionate about it, even if only temporarily.

What about people who are passionate *all* the time? There are several traits that all passionate and successful people have in common.

(1) They have the right relationships, friendships, and networks. They hang around the right people, people who are enthusiastic and optimistic—and they stay away from people who bring them down and are constantly complaining. Those types of people always seem to go nowhere. You know the type of person I'm talking about here.

Invest your time in building bridges with other goal-oriented and successful people who have the same aspirations as you do, who want to make a difference in the world.

Get around big thinkers, or at least put yourself in an environment that is conducive to thinking big. Your life, your business, your perspective—it's all a reflection of how big *you* are. You can choose to always be with people who will challenge you to rise to new levels.

If we spend a lot of time with people who have no vision or goals for their lives, no purpose, no passion, no enthusiasm, we will probably start to be just like them!

However, if you spend your time with people who challenge you to be better, you are making a wise choice.

(2) They expose themselves to the newest and hottest trends and ideas. If I were to ask you how much time you spent each day reading a new magazine, or trying new ideas out, or even doing something as simple as watching a new show on TV, most of you would probably say, "Not much."

But new info, new intellectual input, is essential to keeping the coals of our passion stoked! Get yourself educated! Open your mind and look around you. See what other people are doing to acquire wealth and success. Your senses must have a steady diet of change and innovation in order for you to succeed.

(3) They have goals—which they achieve. Prepare yourself by educating yourself, then going about the process of attaining those goals. Not just talking about it, but *doing it!* Combining learning and setting goals are the surest methods I know to prepare for success. If you don't develop the hunger and courage to pursue your goals, you will lose your nerve and will give up!

I wake up early every day, and that's when I get my best work done—no phones, no distractions, no people, no crying babies, no nothing . . . except for my brain and me. At night, my mind is mush, so mornings are when I do my planning, my goal setting, and my best thinking. Do you spend time each day setting and reviewing your goals, both personal and professional? If not, you need to.

(4) They take advantage of opportunities that come their way. You've no doubt heard someone say, "Boy, she sure is lucky" or "He seems to get all the lucky breaks." I can tell you that hard work, perseverance, and dedication create luck. First, you must learn to recognize it (often it shows up in the form of adversity). Second, act on it. Opportunity is very elusive. It's all over the place, but very few can see it because it usually involves change, which is a very scary thought.

(5) They are willing to take risks and make mistakes. The best teacher I ever had was failure, and believe me I've had more than my fair share of that. But if you learn to look at the mistakes that you make and the failures you have had as learning experiences, you get a whole new perspective on things.

No risk, no reward! Taking chances is a very common thread among the ultra-passionate and successful people in the world. If you want to succeed, you'd better be willing to risk whatever it takes to get it done.

Thomas Edison failed over 6,000 times before he finally invented the light bulb, and Donald Trump has had more than a handful of disasters. I don't think for a minute we would call these people failures, would we? They took risks to better themselves, and things worked out just fine!

(6) They are disciplined and tenacious. Tenacity is different from passion and commitment. It is the perseverance that takes a task through to the end. Edison was tenacious. Passionate people are always disciplined, and undisciplined people are always unpassionate. Disciplined people know that passion *does not* fall into your lap! They know that being impatient will cause you a lot of heartache in life. It is actually one of the root causes of failure, but very few realize it.

Passionate people *don't give up*! In 1908, a marathon runner entered the Olympic stadium and nearly collapsed from exhaustion. During the last part of the race, he fell time and time again before one of the officials finally helped him across the finish line. Obviously, he was disqualified, but he became an instant international star.

Then there was the runner from Great Britain who was hobbled by a torn hamstring about half way through the 1992 Olympic marathon. As he entered the stadium, his father jumped out of the stands to help his son, and he hopped the rest of the way to the finish line. Talk about an inspirational moment.

Another example of courage and perseverance in the face of adversity is the Tasmanian runner whose leg was bleeding and bandaged as he staggered into the Olympic stadium more than an entire hour behind the rest of his competitors in the 1968 Olympic marathon. He later said, "My country did not send me here to start the race, they sent me here to finish the race." .

(7) Passionate people are continuously educating themselves—and applying what they learn. Let's talk about the education process for just a minute. We've all been to seminars and workshops where we've gotten so fired up that we couldn't wait to get home and implement the ideas. Many of us have read a book that touched us in a powerful way or watched a video that opened up our minds to some new and creative technique. Perhaps you are thinking of an occasion or two at this moment.

What happens when you return home? If you are like most other people in this world, usually nothing. All those fantastic life-altering ideas overflowing in our brains and in our notebooks often lead to nothing. The notebook gets put into the "notebook closet" that we all have in the back room that has no light, where the only things growing are mold, mildew, and mushrooms!

Our brains get filled up with the chaos of life: kids, cars, grocery shopping, the weather, practice, games, mowing the lawn, employees, receivables and payables, vacations, and everything else that competes for our thoughts, and we forget about the life-altering ideas that our notebook contained.

A Secret about Education and Learning: How They Happen

Education and learning are like hearing a song on the radio. If you hear a song and you like it, you want to hear it again. If you hear it five times, you can sing along. If you hear it ten times, you can sing it on your own without the music. If you want to become a master at these techniques, ten times is the key.

The point, you ask? Good habits take time to create, and bad habits take time to break. Commit yourself to reading every important book you can get your hands on, watching every DVD you can find, listening to every tape and CD you come across, and going to seminars and workshops that focus on making you better!

CHAPTER 13

Mitche's 5-Step Program

There is no quick fix or magic wand I can wave, or potion I can give you that will give you the success you are dreaming for. The recipe is contained in a secret formula that I am about to give you. Grab a pen, and get ready for me to rock your world. Are you ready? Come a little closer . . . closer. Okay, here it is: There are no secrets! Surprise! But there are some techniques.

Mitche's 5-Step Program

Would you like to reinvent your life? If you are diligent with implementing the following steps, I guarantee that you will energize and invigorate your creative juices and give yourself a whole new perspective! I will tell you right now that it won't be easy, but if you are dedicated with your follow-through, it may be the best thing that has ever happened to you!

The Passionate Life

Living the passionate life is not easy! If it were, our entire world would be much better off! But it's not. It takes a very special person to keep their nose to the grindstone each and every day, through good days and bad. My goal for you is that you will begin to replace the negative habits in your life with positive, productive habits that will bring extra richness to your sense of purpose. The end goal is to make these steps part of your everyday routine. I challenge you to take this project seriously; you will reap the rewards and begin living an energized and productive life.

Step 1: Take an Inventory

This will actually be fun once you get into the swing of it. To start with, you will need to make yourself a promise that you will be brutally honest. Since this is an exercise for your eyes only, there really isn't any risk involved, so go ahead and let your defenses down for a bit.

If you are a business owner, you know the joy of doing inventory at the end of each month. This is similar: At the end of the process, you will have a firm grasp on everything that is inside of your "Life Warehouse." There are no right or wrong answers; it's only information. The more information you have about yourself, the better equipped you will be to create the kind of life that you have always wanted.

We need to be acutely aware of who we are and what motivates us, and spending time with yourself is an important part of the process. Grab a pen, a notepad, and a good cup of coffee, and hit your back deck for a while.

You are going to break your life down into three categories: Personal, family, and professional. This exercise is basically intended to get your life, as it exists today, onto a piece of paper:

- Are you satisfied with your physical appearance? Have you been meaning to begin your New Year's exercise program but have been sidetracked with life's other pressing issues? Do you get upset at yourself for not sticking to your diet or to your exercise program?

- Are you satisfied with your spiritual growth? Do you attend church services as much as you would like?

- What hobbies are you involved in? Do you spend as much time as you would like participating in these hobbies, or have they been put on the back burner? Are you spending as much time "alone" as you would like, or has that time been sucked up by life's little emergencies?

- Have you given up some of your passions, perhaps because of children or because of your career?

What are they, and would you want to make them part of your life again?

- What do you like about yourself?

- What don't you like about yourself?

The purpose of this exercise is to "rattle your brain" a little bit to get the cobwebs out! Once you have brainstormed about your life as it exists today, it's time to give some thought about where you want your life to be tomorrow!

Step 2: Brainstorm!

Grab a stack of 3x5 cards and let the creative juices flow! You are going to write down your goals for the next 12 months—your personal, professional, and family goals. The first will be the list of your personal goals, which should be done before the others. Once you figure out what you want out of your life, the rest will come easily!

The Passionate Life

Do you want to take a vacation, or two, or three this year? Do you have your eye on a special boat or set of golf clubs? How about your garden? Would you like to spend more time cultivating it or working in the yard? What about other hobbies you may have, but haven't made time for recently? If it's important to you, then you should make the time in your schedule to read, or write, or paint, or play with the family dog.

Write down one goal/creative idea per note card. What projects have you been meaning to start, or finish? Where do you want to be in one month, three months, a year, five years? What new hobbies do you want to learn? What old hobbies and interests would you like to bring back into your life? Have you been meaning to start that New Year's diet? What projects have you been putting off because you just didn't have the time? Where do you want to go on vacation this year, next year, the year after? What about your family? Would you like to spend more quality time with each of them individually? *Write it all down on a note card.*

You may have an entire stack of things you've been "meaning to get to" but have not dedicated the necessary time.

Procedural note: This exercise must be done at a time and place where you won't be interrupted or distracted. Passion-driven people are not born; they are developed. And by spending just 15 minutes a day immersed in setting goals for your life and brainstorming, you will begin to create positive habits that will stick with you for the rest of your life! Once you come up with an idea, *write it down*! After you put it on paper, it will be much easier to expand the idea and develop it into creative breakthroughs.

Step 3: Prioritize (The Salsa Box)

Now that you have a stack of goals and aspirations, it's time to set some priorities. If you tried to complete everything in your stack, I would venture to say that you would fail miserably and would get disgusted with yourself in the process. Instead of eating the whole pizza all at once, you need to set some realistic goals.

Categorize your goals into three groups. Goals or projects that you can't wait to get started on can be placed into the "hot" section of your salsa box. Items that are a little more long term can be put into the "medium" category, and things that are long term, or possibly things you may never get to, can be put into the "mild" section.

You can call it your "Salsa Goal Box." That will make it easier to establish some realistic time lines for your goals, and by having everything already written down in your Salsa Goal Box, you will increase the chance that you will be successful!

Step 4: Share

If you want this to truly make a difference in your life, you must become accountable to at least one other living person. It may be your spouse, your business partner, your best friend—someone who understands your motivations and can support you with your new set of eyes. Set a time where you can lay out your game plan and share your goals and aspirations.

Ask the other person to make sure to hold your feet to the fire on occasion so that you don't get lazy. If you set up a monthly "meeting" with him or her to discuss how things are going, you will allow the other person to be involved with your efforts in a very personal way; plus, you will hold yourself accountable to someone besides yourself.

Step 5: Take Action

Once you have established your list of goals and shared them with a confidant, it's time to put your money where your mouth is. Putting some of your goals into motion can be a revolutionary step for you, and once you get the momentum going in your direction—watch out, world! Don't make up excuses or come up with reasons why you *can't* do something. Just go out and get it done. As Nike says, JUST DO IT!

Taking the Initiative…Making Things Happen by Starting Small

As you put my program into action and begin to emulate passionate people, choose something small that you will be able to accomplish easily and dedicate yourself to doing it every day for one week. Maybe it's something as simple as going for a short walk at lunch, or spending 30 minutes every day reading self-improvement books, or going through boxes in your basement, or maybe stopping on the way home to visit a friend who's been feeling down lately.

Once you begin to make these small items part of your daily routine, you will gain momentum, so that the bigger things won't seem quite so daunting and overwhelming. The smallest things can make the biggest difference.

Don't make the mistake of being too busy to do the things you need to do in order to be successful in this task.

CHAPTER **14**

Summing It Up

In a survey of a group of elderly people, one question was, "If you were to live your life again, what would you do different?" Over 95 percent answered that they would reflect more, risk more, and do more things that would live on after they were gone. Isn't that a wonderful perspective? The best part is that we don't have to wait until our life is nearly over before we can begin to live like this. You can begin *today*.

There's nothing sadder to me than when someone doesn't give their life enough value, or when someone says, "I didn't live my life like I should have. I didn't achieve, I didn't take any risks." There's no going back to the beginning of the race.

Every night when we put our head on our pillow and go to sleep, it's one less day that we have. Can you imagine getting up and going to work and having to do things you don't like to do or that you are not very good at? That's not the kind of thing that makes you get up every day with a spring in your step. "Yahoo, I get to go off and do something I don't like to do and I'm not very good at!" It would be quite painful, I would say.

But when you get up with a sense of passion and purpose, and you love what you do, it's going to bring your focus into a very narrow beam of energy. When you get up in the morning, you have literally thousands of things that you could *choose* to do. Thousands! It's the choices we make that will determine the outcome.

Summing It Up: One-Liners

I've talked a lot about what the passionate life is—and is not. Let me sum it up with a few one-liners or two.

- We can't choose when we are born or when our time is up. What we can choose is how we spend our dash.

- At the end of your life, all that matters is who you loved and who loved you. Your legacy. You need to be able to stand by *you* more than anyone else.

- The "X-Factor" is your attitude!

- Life is short! Way too short to not do what you are passionate about.

- Kiss slowly, love truly, and laugh uncontrollably when you can, and never regret anything that made you smile!

The Passionate Life

- Keep your focus on what is truly important in life, do the best that you can with everything that you do, and the rest will fall into place.

- If you love what you do, you will never have to work a day in your life.

- Don't be satisfied with less. Don't become stagnant. Don't settle for "good enough."

- Put yourself in an environment where you can grow. The minute you stop learning is the minute you start dying.

- Constantly ask yourself: Who am I, where am I going, what is life all about, what is my vision for the future?

- You are never too young or too old to dream big dreams.

- Our thoughts determine the direction of our life.

- Life is more about the journey than the destination.

What's holding you back from living the life of your dreams? What steps can you take *today* in order to make those dreams come true? I've noticed that many people in this world do not have a real sense of direction, almost as if they are waiting for someone to show them the way. You must make the choice to move forward with your life and not sit around waiting for the magic to just happen out of the blue.

There are two kinds of people in this world: those who wait for something to happen and those who take the initiative and make things happen. If you need to change, don't make any more excuses! Hoping that things will change has no effect. Only tangible actions on your part will make the difference. You may need to eliminate a few things from your daily to-do list in order to be able to regain your focus on what's truly important.

Life is a very delicate balance. The challenge is to keep your perspective and rediscover or to discover for the first time what's really important to you. We never know when our time is up. What is it that you love to do? What do you get excited about? I believe most people live like they are a bubblegum wrapper in a parking lot, meandering wherever the wind blows. Make sure it's *your* life you're living. You have to believe that you *deserve* to be happy; you have to decide to live life to the fullest.

TODAY MATTERS! Take action today! Don't put off until tomorrow what you can do today. The world is filled with sad, hurting people. Use what you have in your hand to make someone else's life better!

Living Like You Mean It

If you want to make the most of your life and live it with enthusiasm and zeal, reading this book will not be enough. You will need to make decisions along the way. Your approach to life will need to change; so will your attitude and the way you allocate your time.

Any type of transformation requires a process; it requires *change*. We are constantly in the "process" of becoming . . . whatever that means to each one of us. It all is part of our transformation into a better person—leaving our chrysalis and becoming a butterfly.

Will you start that transformation . . .today?

The Passionate Life

This is not the end, but rather the beginning . . .